Brooks Books presents

The Social Media Handbook

An Adult Guide Through the Digital Life of a Teen

Adam Brooks

Copyright © 2016 Adam Brooks
All rights reserved.

ISBN-10: 0-9974585-1-8

ISBN-13: 978-0-9974585-1-0

Dedication

This book is dedicated to all of the parents, educators and community members who didn't grow up with social media but have been trying to learn about it in order to help the young people in their lives. I want you to know that you are not alone in your struggle to learn what you need to know. There are many of us who are fighting to help you make life easier in regards to managing your kids' social media platforms. This book is for you all…Cheers!

Table of Contents

Dedication	2
Preface	4
Introduction	5
The History of Social Media	7
Unintended Consequences	15
Benefits	20
Role Models	25
Video Games	31
Social Media and Guns	38
Boomers vs. Millennials	41
Actual Hardware	46
The Space	49
Tips and Tricks	51
Summing It All Up	64
References	66
Glossary for Technology Norms	67
About the Author	69

Preface

My name is Adam Brooks. I am a first generation college student who has a Bachelor's Degree in Speech Communication as well as a Master's Degree in Special Education and Leadership Development. I am the founder of Youth Awareness and Safety. I coauthored the book *WTF-Why Teens Fail and What to Fix,* and I authored the Brooks Books series, featuring the bestselling mini-book *Understanding Millennials- Tips and Tricks for Working with Today's Generation.*

Along with sitting on the Board of Directors at New Way Academy school, I was a seasonal administrator at Texas Lions Camp. As a former high school educator and current adjunct professor, I talk to audiences about topics ranging from bullying to body image.

Introduction

A study given to the President of the United States by the Department of Economics stated that our teens and younger generation touch their cell phones to check updates over 45 times per day.

The term social media has become commonplace and not just in the mouths of Millennials but also in the business, educational and nonprofit worlds. Companies have even had to create new jobs to handle their social media postings. Social media is a hot topic today, and we need to get a handle on it if we are going to keep ourselves and our kids safe in this digital culture that we find ourselves in.

Phrases like cyber-bullying, sexting and even digital footprint are being thrown around, and yet we don't know what to do about them. We have to begin the discussion of how to help our teens and ourselves walk through this online world. That is what this mini-book is all about, starting that conversation for you and your families. For those of us that are older than 35, we may be unsure of what it's like growing up with technology infused into every aspect of our lives. Technology wasn't as prevalent for us as it is for those trying to grow up today and figure out where they fit in this society.

Read this book with open and responsive eyes. When we think about our students and teens, give them grace when it comes to social media. They are experiencing things that we never thought would be an issue when we were growing up. We are in uncharted territory in a lot of ways when it comes to everything online, so we must make our way carefully. Let this be a guide to help you know where to start. My company, Youth Awareness and Safety, has a saying: "Start smart, start small, but just start!" If we take the first steps into this messy, weird, awesome and social media-driven life, we will never regret it, and we will be an amazing resource for our kids.

I hope you enjoy the mini-book.

The History of Social Media

There is some debate about the beginning of social media. There are a lot of similarities between our current use of social media and the way people gathered in common areas to discuss the issues of the day in ancient times. Whether it be gathering around a cave wall watching someone draw pictures or walking around the agora in ancient Greece discussing the political and social issues of the time, people have always gathered in a sharing of minds. It was common in ancient Greece for people, especially men, to head to the marketplace to walk with other men and discuss a variety of issues. Rhetoric and public speaking played such an important role in ancient Greece that groups used the agora as places to show off their knowledge and their superior debating and communication skills. This isn't completely unlike today's social media experts.

We eventually created the Cracker Barrel, a concept where people gathered in shops around barrels of crackers and caught up on what was new in their lives.

If we follow the timeline further, we see letter writing enabling people to connect with one another over great distances. Then we see the telegraph and the radio which were ways that mass communication could finally touch all corners of our world.

We don't see the first digital connections start to take place until the late 1970s, with the dawning of email and chat rooms. But all of these things have lead us to where we stand today with social media platforms. Facebook, Instagram, Twitter, Periscope,

Vine, Snapchat, Kik, WhatsApp—all of these are simply digital versions of the ancient agora!

The father of our most recent social media-type experiences is surprisingly LinkedIn, which was started in 2002. It was started as a way to view resumes and discuss business issues. This trend caught on very quickly because every year after, until 2006, another social media site popped up. Instant messenger got really popular in the 90's which brought about many issues we will talk about later in this mini-book. In 2003, Myspace began, which was a full year before Facebook. Myspace became a fast success, and it took off more than was first anticipated. Designed as a way for small-town music and bands to get accessed by the mainstream, Myspace allowed people to connect and stay connected on a social level.

The Facebook story has become one of the most popular stories told in the tech world, and having a movie written about the rise of the company doesn't hurt. Facebook came on the scene in 2004 and set the bar for social media. Once it took off, it paved the way in innovation, leading to other websites and applications using Facebook to spin off their own versions and styles of social connection.

My own history with social media may be similar to yours. I grew up typing papers in elementary and middle school on a typewriter while learning about computers and technology in school. However, email had still not quite caught up to our educational institutions. We were still playing *Where in the World is Carmen San Diego?* (if you are from my generation you sang that last line) on a real-life floppy disk or even *Oregon Trail* where we all kept dying of dysentery. We continually practiced our home row typing skills while others, who got done faster, got to play *Sim City* and create their own vast metropolises. However, if we wanted to talk to someone we still had to meet them at the slide on the playground or find them on the basketball court. We may have been able to call them at home, but that was always problematic since the phone cord was connected to the wall and had about a five-foot walking radius. That meant that our parents could hear our entire conversation, and they had plenty of questions as soon as we were done talking. (Ugh, even back then, parents were all up in our business!)

It was about the middle of high school before there was a computer in our home. All of those times we had begged to get a computer so that "turning in home work papers would be easier" had finally paid off. At first, all I seemed to use it for was to play games. On the weekends, I got to kill bad guys on *Wolfenstein*. Once we got the dial-up capability to actually run the Internet, a whole new world opened up at our house. The sound of the computer trying to connect to our one and only phone line was a strange-sweet music to my ears. My parents would check their email (they probably checked it once a week or once every other week back then), and as soon as they were done, I got to get on AIM Instant Messenger and wait to see if any of my friends were there as well. If they were, I would try and chat with them, see what they were up to...I knew what they were up to: they were sitting in front of their family computer like me!

Our home computer was just a small introduction, because when I left to go to college (a few hours north) every dorm room had a computer or laptop. All of them connected with what was called Ethernet, which meant for the first time in my life I could have a phone connection AND an Internet connection! MIND BLOWN!!

The Internet was the easiest way to talk to my friends across campus. We could chat online while we were "working" on writing papers or while we were doing online research for other projects. This made the hard work and difficulty of school much easier to cope with, because while I was complaining about my rhetoric class, Laurie was complaining to me about her Spanish class. Not only did this build camaraderie but it gave a whole new dimension to "study buddies" since we could actually study from separate rooms.

> *In any given month, approximately 1.28 BILLION people are active on Facebook —roughly equivalent to the entire population of India, the world's second most-populous country.*
>
> –Social Media Networking Report
> (Shewan, 2017)

Smart phones had come out during this time, but they were still crazy-expensive, and most of us college kids in the early days didn't have one. I borrowed my parents "emergency" cell phone once, called a friend, and that one phone call cost them…ok it cost me, $45! But by the time I was a senior in college (23 years old), I had my own cell phone that I paid for each month, and I could even text my friends (but only with the dreaded T9). Technology was moving faster and faster.

How fast does technology move, I wonder?

The radio was invented in the early 1900s. The first few radio transmissions were sent out around 1910, and as WWI raged on, the transmissions got more prevalent. However, the radio didn't catch on until the "golden age of radio", which refers to the 1920s through the 1950s. It took nearly a decade for the radio to catch on enough for people to want one in their homes for entertainment and news and for the electronics to become accessible.

The television was invented around the same time as the radio; however, because it had more moving parts and took so much longer to create, the TV didn't catch on until the early- to mid-1950s. Even then, it didn't become a household item until around 10 years later since they were still quite expensive. However, the time between the black and white TV and the color TV was less than 10 years. The technology kept improving on both the radio and the television. After 1950, we see technology take some humongous leaps forward…soon after, we went to the MOON!

Every technological advance seems to be accepted by the public quicker and quicker. Once pagers came out in the early 1990s, they were soon (in a matter of 5 years) replaced by cell phones. Cell phones went from bulky heavy one-option things to handheld computers in no time flat. Now, as soon as the newest iPad is out, people know how to use it and are waiting in line for it.

This adjustment on how we see and use our technology has huge implications on our desire to have the next and greatest device that can somehow "make our lives better." Think about all the ways our lives have changed that don't even have to do with the device itself, such as the invention of the TV dinner and the need for an entertainment cabinet in the home.

We have devices for our devices; our phones now need applications to enhance them. It just seems never-ending: the amount of things that have changed or we now do differently because of some sort of device that is either bringing us together or keeping us apart.

Television was such a huge thing for my household growing up that I found myself sneaking out of my room and standing in the hallway for hours, just to catch glimpses of what my parents watched after us kids went to bed! When I stayed home sick from school, I would just sit and (for hours and hours) watch all the silly daytime television that my grandparents loved so much.

Obsessing over technology, or making it a priority, really isn't anything new. People have reserved times and dates for exciting events such as, *Fireside Radio* chats with the President, *Wheel of Fortune*, soap operas or telenovelas, or even the *Bachelor* was written into people's calendars as an event. People made sacrifices to witness these things much like people do for other events today: waiting in line for the new iPhone or watching the season premiere of *Game of Thrones*.

We can only imagine what tomorrow will bring with it. Already, we have Google Glasses, voice-automated phones and even cars that park and drive themselves. Our technology is getting increasingly more advanced, and we are unsure about all of the unexpected consequences. The consequences of how far our technology has already come are something we are just starting to realize, and if we don't take action quickly, we may be too late.

Unintended Consequences

I decided in college to minor in sociology. I enjoyed both psychology and sociology, but really the study of how we act as groups fascinated me! Something changes when we are with people; it's different than when we are alone. It's amazing what large groups of people are capable of, good and bad. The novel *The Outsiders* was written in 1967, and yet the premise of two groups of students, the Socs and the Greasers, who are continually fighting each other, is still one that students can relate to today. Their story is about social classes and being from different backgrounds. The kind of stuff that anyone from any time period can relate to.

So, imagine putting all of these groups of kids online and giving them little to no supervision or direction on how to use their online presence. You've got the same group mentality with none of the actual repercussions, because they aren't talking in person. This is a great way to give people the ability to say whatever they want without the actual ownership of those words. When we use a medium like a computer, or a pencil and paper, or even a phone, it takes away an aspect of life, or the soul, because it is happening through technology, which in and of itself is soulless. This is essentially the issue with online relationships.

Technology was created to bring people closer together and make it easier to communicate. The unintended consequence is that, over time, it became such a popular way to communicate that we have come close to forgetting the need for actual soul connection. Today's students have had so much time communicating online that they forget to sit down face-to-face with people. When they finally do sit down face-to-face, many young people aren't sure what to do. This frustration has led to tons of young people choosing to get rid of their phones, or to not use them as frequently, because they have made a genuine connection to others, and they want to keep having it. They recognize what those of us who grew up without those means of communication always knew: with genuine connection comes healthier relationships.

Let's look at a common issue facing young people today: bullying (in fact, even some of us older people face it as well.) This issue has taken on a new aspect...I'm not talking about the "I'm going to take your lunch money" type of bully. Nah, what we are talking about is something much more awful. I call it harassment, although others have called it cyber-bullying. These terms have been used and reused and overused so much that I'm afraid they are losing their actual meaning. A kid gets called a name at school, (e.g., loser) and when that kid gets home, back in my day, he would tell his parents, "Someone called me a loser at school today." His parents would reassure him, saying, "Well, you know you aren't a loser." And typically, that was where it would end.

However, today, a kid gets called a loser at school and then when he gets home, his phone goes off and someone else has called him a loser, or someone adds a hurtful comment on Instagram, or someone sends a Snapchat making fun of him somehow. There becomes no safe place for this kid, because his phone and computer are going off at home with just as many hurtful things as he heard at school that day.

> *Online is old news. Online in social media is today's news...social media is not a subset of the internet. Social media is the Internet.*
>
> *-Sean Case (Shewan, 2017)*

Whenever someone has no safe place, it is easy to understand why they would go to drastic measures to get it to stop. It could be by hurting themselves or it could be hurting someone else. Either way, the end result is pain, because we are forgetting to ground our kids and give them that soulful connection they are so desperately crying out for.

Another issue we come across is predators. Because so many of our kids are dying for a real connection, there are key words and phrases that people can use online to really get the attention of lonely children. When someone wants to do those kids harm, it is not hard for a predator to figure out what angle to take to talk to these kids so that they feel comfortable enough to start oversharing information, and before we know it, harm happens to those kids. This is why discussing these things is incredibly important, so that we can learn how to teach and protect our kids against things like this. It is an ever-growing problem, and the biggest issue is that those of us who didn't grow up on social media and technology really don't know what to do, because these weren't issues during our childhood. The issue that was most similar to our time was not getting into a stranger's van, even if we were offered candy.

This is why the crux of fighting bullying, or even cyber-bullying, has less to do with just telling kids "Stop it!" and more to do with building up the self-confidence kids need to withstand words, comments, pictures and whatever else gets thrown their way. If we can teach resiliency, then we are able to build strong youth who can overcome whatever gets thrown at them.

We can't talk about the unintended consequences of social media and leave out the variety of decision-making issues that they will encounter online. It isn't just mean girls they have to look out for, and it isn't just predators. Those are the extremes of what you see online. Really, the main issue that I have found with students is much subtler. It's what one student referred to as being a *double agent*, when you post things that you think others would want to hear, but they aren't who you are or what you want to represent. I have seen students who have great character and who know themselves well that make poor decisions online that ended up hurting them later.

It's by making those small decisions to comment something inappropriate on a friend's post or send a picture that some may see as unhealthy or hurtful that result in people looking at them differently, that confuses our kids. This generation, more than any other, has a hard time realizing that they can brand themselves online, and that they can ruin their lives by destroying their reputation. This concept of perception is reality is a difficult one for young people to understand. They want truth to be truth and everyone else's perception of them be damned. However, we know that is exactly the issue. If they don't want to be known as someone who does drugs, they need to not post about drugs. This perception online is not something that most students realize is going to be an issue. That's why it's an unintended consequence.

Benefits

Now that we have discussed some of the negative consequences of social media, let's look at the positives and the reasons why it can be really helpful—not only for teens and our youth but also for some of our own societal needs.

> *44% of all Twitter accounts have never sent a tweet.*
>
> **-Twopchart
> (Shewan, 2017)**

For the first time in the history of the world, we are totally connected. I mean totally connected. I have traveled through the hills of Turkey and seen small villages, and they all had cell phones! Any one of us could pick up a cell phone and (in theory) call almost anywhere in the world and talk to that other person instantaneously. That is simply incredible. Things like the telegraph and letter writing have become novelty items that can still be used but only out of preference not out of necessity. The ramifications and impact of this really seem to be endless. We can get current up-to-date information about issues happening around the globe. We can even provide help financially or by raising awareness from all the way around the world.

Nothing proves this better than the ALS Water Challenge that swept the Internet a few years ago, which raised more money for Amyotrophic Lateral Sclerosis than any other fundraising in the history of The ALS Association. The fact that I can text a number and donate a dollar to any given charity is an example of the good that can come from social media. It has never been so easy to affect change and actually see that change! In the past, we would try and start a movement or create change, and we just sort of hoped that it worked, only to discover years later that it really didn't help. Today, we can instantly know if something is working or not…we have immediate feedback. So why shouldn't we try innovative ideas? This is the perfect time to do exactly that.

I know that one of the arguments about how frustrating this generation can be is that they are too vulnerable. Millennials will divulge their deepest and darkest secrets to anyone who asks them, especially when it is online because they don't have to face anyone…it feels simply anonymous, like writing in a journal. The positive side to that, however, is that they are learning to be vulnerable…they are learning to be honest with what they feel. These things can be hugely important in life. For someone who grew up with a family that wasn't always open about what they were feeling…those Polish Catholics can be pretty secretive about what they really think… I have found that this is a really refreshing trait. I agree it is not always positive, but it still seems like they have a leg up emotionally on previous generations.

I want to paint an alternative picture…

Imagine this:

A college that I am applying to after high school asks me the question, "Tell me about yourself." As a teen who has had a social media experience for the past 3 years, I have a documented history of all the things that I have done educationally as well as in the community. I can look back and show the school, with pictures included, exactly who I am and what I am all about. That is one reason that social media has very exciting potential. We could truly allow a university to see all the amazing things we have done and give them a better peek into the lives of the students they are accepting.

The main issue with this is that if the student is not using social media to positively brand herself, but rather to inadvertently hurt her image. I don't mean that any other type of social media besides branding brings about bad results. When I say *hurt themselves* I am referring to the stereotypical issue that I have run into as an educator where drama, bullying and harassment are all becoming digital in nature. That is why education is so important. Imagine if a student went into high school realizing that Twitter, Instagram and Facebook were tools for branding. They came out of school with a clear picture of their life passion and had a visual and written collection of all the great things they accomplished as well as the difficulties that they had to overcome. Wouldn't that be a great testament of what they could bring into a University or even into any community that they were choosing to be a part of? I think this is a great way to focus on the beauty of social media. It does take work and training, but it is completely attainable.

Positive Conflict

Sometimes we think of conflict online or digital issues as being very negative and we take it out on social media. We believe it should be avoided at all costs. I have to say that I couldn't disagree more. I think that one of the major benefits is that there is, and can be, conflict on social media for our teens. The main issue is when we leave them alone to handle it all by themselves. Or we allow them to go to their fellow teens for advice. I love when teens find community. However, when they are each other's primary source of information, you find tons of misinformation and bad choices. We have to be the ones that walk through those conflicts with these teens. Conflict online can be extremely useful to teach teens a few things when we allow them to risk within the safety that we can provide.

Conflict helps us start to think, "I don't think I agree with them." It is the start of an in-depth internal conversation, where we begin to discover what we (ourselves) actually think about something. It really helps us build a belief system and decide what we want in future friends and relationships. The main issue is when we don't flesh these lessons out and discuss them with our teen. Conflict can feel hard and sad when we don't get a glimpse of the bigger picture and see the healthier and better situation it brings about. Conflict is the thing that helps us see ourselves as individuals…if we miss out on capitalizing on that conflict, which will inevitably happen, we are missing a valuable tool and teaching opportunity.

> *Girls are more likely to dominate social media, while boys prefer video games.*
>
> - Pew Research Center (Shewan, 2017)

Role Models

When I was growing up, my role models included political figures, actors and actresses, and athletes. I even remember begging my parents for sunglasses just like my idol, Ryne Sandberg, the Chicago Cubs second baseman who would flip up or down his sunglasses depending on where the sun and baseball was. I watched his games and collected as many of his baseball cards as I could find. If I ever saw him in person, I am not sure how I would have reacted, but I can guarantee you that cool and calm would not have been the adjectives I would use. Today, our students and teens have a whole new type of role model. Welcome to the day and age of the Internet celebrity!

I was talking with a friend of mine, whose daughter has just started using social media—nothing too crazy, just Instagram and musical.ly, really. The daughter just wants to talk to her friends and enjoys making music videos with the app. One of the things that my friend has noticed is that her daughter, we will call her Cindy, is becoming mildly obsessed with people who are using social media. YouTube videos are a great example. There are many YouTube *celebrities* who have millions of followers. These people have made a living and a life using social media. Saying someone is Instagram famous or YouTube famous is actually legitimate and means something. There are people all over the world who are watching what people do online and either learning from it, laughing because of it or wanting to be like it. Several documentaries have been made about these Internet celebrities and their rise to stardom.

It all started when Cindy asked her mom if she could go to a concert featuring YouTube singers. YouTube singers are people who haven't technically "made it" in Hollywood; they simply have a ton of followers and started selling tickets to shows that they put on around the country. We aren't talking just small little venues; we are talking 400 people at 50 bucks a person. This is a pretty major undertaking for people who are just on YouTube singing. These "celebrities" are making, in some cases, six-figure incomes just making several minute videos of themselves talking or joking about their life or experiences. There is even a woman who opens plastic eggs and finds toys inside of them. She takes the toys out and plays with them…most of my nieces and nephews and children I know seem mesmerized by this whole process.

So is this a good or a bad thing?

That is a valid question, and I think the answer is more complex than just good or bad.

We live in a day and age when everyone has a voice. It can be a really inspiring thing to hear some of the stories that these people tell. It can also be incredible that someone can easily YouTube "how to fix a sink" and find several videos with the very answer they are looking for. This can really help build connections and allow people to see that they aren't alone. Our teens can go to these videos and see that other people feel the same way. Or get advice on a topic that they are too shy to ask about. The possibilities are endless.

As a networker, this sort of stuff gets me very excited. I have been a motivational speaker for quite some time now, and that means that anyone can check out my speeches and things I talk about with the click of a button. I can send those videos across the country and get new, exciting speaking engagements just from what they see in those videos. It is easy access to the masses, regardless of talent or what you want to say. There are quite a few professionals that I follow on social media because I admire them and want to see what they are up to or what advice they are giving. I subscribe to their YouTube channel and follow them on Twitter. It really does give me the illusion that I know them. And when I interact on their account and they write back or make a comment on what I said, there is a sense of satisfaction and excitement that comes with it. So I totally understand when teens or kids follow someone online that they like and get excited when they get to interact with them, even if it is online…and even if the account is run by a social media company and not by the "celebrity."

The negative impact is that there is an endless supply of videos, and people who are making them, on YouTube, Twitter and Instagram. Not all of them are helpful and meaningful. There is a big risk that some of these people are not sharing the values that we want in our teens. So to have access to so much material, and to have it all unfiltered by those who care about the student, seems like a big risk.

Letting our students and kids take advice from some random person on the Internet is quite a bit scary. There is everything from cat videos to people talking about their sex lives. Only some of these videos and these video creators get to what is considered celebrity status. Those that do, get millions of views and likes on their social media accounts. This idolization of regular people has reinforced the notion that anyone can be someone famous or important. Now that these people have reached this status, younger generations are going to them to listen to their opinions on politics, religion and society as a whole. To be honest, when I was a kid we did the same thing with actors, musicians and athletes. However, this is on a whole new level of intensity with no censorship and no public relations company ensuring that the message is correct and something worthy of sharing.

Cindy, our little friend who loves to follow famous Instagram and YouTube celebrities (in her world), was out and about in town and saw one of those very people she follows at a restaurant. She was so awestruck and excited about seeing that person that she couldn't eat or concentrate. She was way too embarrassed to say anything…I mean what if they knew she was the one liking and commenting on all their posts? Cindy wasn't able to be present at the dinner table at all.

I know the feeling. It is, basically, how I felt when I was having coffee in Hollywood and the guy who died in like Episode 4 of the show *Sons of Anarchy* was sitting next to me. I kept glancing over to make sure it was him, looking for an opportunity to say something. I mean saying "Hi" wouldn't sound stupid right? I could tell him that I liked his work…or….

yeah, I didn't say a word! If this is the response of a grown man, imagine how it felt for Cindy!

> ***Two new users join LinkedIn every second.***
>
> **-LinkedIn Official Blog (Shewan, 2017)**

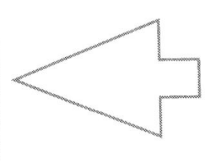

It isn't the celebrity status that I have any issue with in regards to people on social media. Even after I do school assemblies, I get asked by students if they can follow me on my Instagram. I tell them "yes", and they say things like, "Oh wow, look how many followers you have; you're Instagram famous." For them, famous just means a lot of followers and people they interact with.

For me, the part that makes me more nervous is that someone might be giving advice or talking about what they know to be true and teens or students may want to copy them. Students are wanting to copy what they see in the media, and sometimes these things aren't the healthiest things to mimic. This is the part that I am not keen on. In my humble opinion, this sort of thing seems to cause the younger generation to want to grow up faster than the previous ones. With makeup tutorials and YouTube stars talking about various adult topics that vary from drugs to sex to buying the newest and greatest toy, it has a tendency to create what I call the *not good enough* tendency. These commercials (if you will) leave us feeling like we aren't good enough as we are, and that we need something to make us better, whether it is how we do our makeup, the topics we experience or the stuff we own or want to own. These topics are better left to be discussed by families and trusted adults, which is hard to regulate. When our students have free time and free reign to watch and listen to whoever, and whatever, they want, it makes it a bit dicey on the quality of information they are getting.

I will say, and this will be my last point, if you know your student or kid watches or follows one of these so-called celebrities, follow along yourself. Or watch the YouTube videos together. This could be a great bonding opportunity or, at the very least, you will know what is being said so that you can make sure that you are able to give your two cents as well. That way, you are able to participate in what your kid is learning and can add your wisdom to the conversation…even if it is just casually while you are driving in the car.

Video Games

A discussion on social media would not be complete without a section on video game usage and the way that it plays into the socialization of our students and children. With the rise of video games and the advancement of technology, we are now able to play games "live" where we spend time talking to people online while we play or even record ourselves playing for others to watch. Yes, people really do watch other people play video games, it has actually become something that people can get paid to do…live stream their game performances. When I was a kid this was called "waiting for your turn." Taking turns would have been the only reason that I would have watched someone else play.

I still remember the day that I got a Nintendo (notice how there are no letters or numbers after that statement). It was Christmas, and my parents had saved up to buy the family a Nintendo. To say that we were excited is an understatement. At the time, a Nintendo was more for a family because there were games like Wheel of Fortune and running pad you could use to compete in Olympic-style events. We still have similar things today with games that belong to devices like the Nintendo Wii. More common now, is the PlayStation empire that has numerous games that a single player can play online, talking to their friends over a headset.

When I was growing up, video games were mainly intended for males…however, in the last five to ten years the amount of females who have started gaming and being a part of the gaming culture has grown dramatically. This means that more and more of our children are getting involved, in some way, in the gaming process.

In addition to an increased number of people playing video games, there's an increase in the number of hours that individuals spend playing. Sometimes, the number of hours spent gaming becomes compulsory and is viewed as addictive in behavior. As of right now, video gaming addiction is not currently in the DSM IV for mental disorders or addictions. However, in 2013, they did get permission to begin studying the addiction to see if it can be added to future editions. So, even though it is not considered officially a disorder, it is on its way to becoming a full-fledged addiction in our society that we may need rehab centers for and the like. Even now, countless rehab facilities receive requests from parents for services for kids who seem to have a video game addiction.

I have to say, though, right up front, that I don't view video gaming or video games as inherently negative. In general, they are totally fine and normal. Video games even produce healthy hormones in the teens and tweens that play them. Kids experience positive feelings of success when they win in the game, and they learn how to problem solve when trying to figure out where to go and what to do. There is even research out there that states that playing video games helps with brain development and memory (Vitelli, 2014). These are great things that young students should be working on and figuring out. Just like anything else in this world, it only becomes negative or an issue when there is excess. Whenever someone has too much of any particular thing, it can create negative consequences. Video gaming is no different. Talk to any eye doctor or chiropractor, and you will see that screen time is affecting our kids and our families. The amount of time a child spends sitting in front of any type of screen: television, computer, phone, iPod, iPad, i-Whatever it really matters.

My Concerns About Excessive Video Games:

1. The amount of time spent playing without proper nutrition or breaks.

Whenever a student binge-games for hours on end the result is never a positive one. Usually, they are locked away in a room playing for hours and not eating healthy, assuming that they are taking breaks to eat at all. So, there is a health factor that comes into play for me as a teacher. I have watched students eat a steady diet of hot Cheetos and convenience store sodas. This always changed their energy, as well as their work ethic, in the classroom.

2. The amount of time spent playing can lead to addiction which becomes a very hard cycle to break.

Most kids love gaming so much, because it stimulates the pleasure and rewards centers of their brains. The more this stimulates that part of their brains, the more they can become addicted to those feelings. Now does that mean that every child who plays video games or even plays for multiple hours is addicted? No. I don't believe so, and it doesn't seem like the research says that either. However, the more they play the more they run the risk of becoming addicted.

A few parents have told me horror stories about their children spending hours playing video games. When the children finally come out of their rooms, they are angry and nasty to their siblings, or they don't want to talk at all. Their minds seem to be crashing after stimulating the reward center of their brains for hours on end. Other times, the kid gets in trouble, and the parents try to take away the gaming device or restrict it in some way. This has led to epic meltdowns, or even, if you look at a few random news reports, made children react violently. There are extreme cases of children attacking their parents when games or devices were taken away. I don't think these are the norm, but they are very concerning to me.

3. Kids are talking over a wireless stream while playing video games; do you know who your kids are talking to?

This is also a concern of mine. When people are gaming online, they can play with people from all over the world. That is something that I never thought would be possible. I understand why kids are so excited to play. They can talk to people from anywhere and play with them or against them. It's fun and adventurous. Whenever I have talked to kids about this, I would ask them who they were talking to and playing against. They typically respond with the same thing every time; "Oh, just some kid." But was it? How did they know? With a lot of these games you can play with anyone on the Internet, so it is a perfect breeding ground for predation. Any person, regardless of age, can talk to our kids and pretend to be any age that they want to. They could be talking and playing with the same kids day after day, and at some point, they may want to meet up. I have plenty of friends who have said that they know that their kid is talking to other kids online, and it's all kid stuff and very innocent. That may be the case for most of the kids...however, it only takes one!

I feel the need to put a disclaimer here, I am a user of social media. I am not a user of video games. I mean, like I mentioned earlier, I did get the original Nintendo for Christmas as a kid, and I played that thing until the buttons barely worked. However, it only had two buttons...Once games started having four or five buttons and getting more and more complicated, I was in a different place in my life. Videogames were no longer something I valued or played. Most of what I know about video games today comes from friends who play, students I know who play, studies I have read, or parents I've talked to.

My suggestions for the parents of gamers:

1. Make sure kids eat healthy snacks and meals regardless of whether or not they are gaming.

We forget sometimes that these teens/tweens are still growing. They need proper nutrition, not just in general, but also because they are physically inactive while they are playing video games. If they are sitting that still, for that many hours, there is a good chance they are not getting the type of food their body needs. Some kids are super active, they run around and play sports, and in those cases, they can typically eat whatever they want because they are burning calories so quickly. Some of these kids are the same, they play outside and they play on video games they can do both, and the majority of the kids I know fall into this category. However, some kids, all they want to do is play video games all day, every day, and those are the kids that really need our help.

2. We need to push time limits on how long our kids can play these video games.

If they play them for too long it numbs their reward centers. Like I mentioned earlier, playing them does have its benefits, so I'm not opposed to them playing at all. However, making sure that it is within the proper time limits is the key. I am wary of giving you a time limit that would be best…every child is different. Some kids at 13-years-old are very mature and can handle more time online gaming. There are also some kids who, at 13-years-old, are immature and really can't handle much more than an hour of gaming online. So, you need to test the water and see…it's always easier to start with low time limits, and add to them if they prove to you they can handle it. If you start with too much time, it is very difficult to pull back later without a big backlash.

3. Put the game console in a central location.

The main suggestion I give to families is that wherever the most traffic is in your house (wherever the carpet is most used and beaten down) that is where you need to have the video game console placed. The issue I see with kids having video games in their rooms, behind closed doors, is that there is really no way to monitor who they are talking to and how long they have been talking to them. For me, wearing a headset is not a right, it is a privilege. And a kid would have to earn a headset from me, once I listened to how they interacted with people in the living room, or the dining room or whatever public place they played at. I would want to hear all the chatter on those video games, even if I don't like it, because than at least we can sit down and talk about what I heard and what they think is appropriate and inappropriate. Keep in mind that punishing your kid for something someone else says does not build trust or support with your own child. So, hear it all, but choose wisely about when you need to intervene.

So, now you know about my concerns, as well as my suggestions, when it comes to video games. These suggestions are just a place to start for those parents or adults that have seen their kids becoming alarmingly obsessed with playing video games. The quicker that we can learn how to limit their access and start to help them cope, the less of a fight it will be later on. The video game industry is one of the fastest growing, so please beware and be on guard. Video gaming can be great fun and meaningful but only when done correctly.

Social Media and Guns

I grew up in Arizona, so the subject of guns is nothing new; we have a lot of guns. However, the subject of Second Amendment rights isn't exactly what I mean to discuss. Gun rights are an incredibly hot topic, but for me, it is not the focus of this section. If I do want to be a gun owner though, or let's just say that I have guns in my home, I would never just hand a loaded gun to a kid and tell them, "Hey, here you go, figure it out! Oh, but don't hurt yourself." Sounds crazy, right? Insane even? It is because nobody would give a kid a loaded gun, hoping that she doesn't hurt herself. Instead, what do we do? We pay for kids to take classes, and we sit around and talk about the seriousness of it. We even lock it away when we aren't using it because it is for a time and a place. Guns become something so important and serious that we make sure our kids understand the importance. We go to the shooting range to practice so that we all understand the importance of safety and when and how to use this powerful device.

I know that this metaphor may be lacking in many ways, but (in many instances) a phone and social media are the same thing. We don't really train our kids on how to use the phone or even how to use social media. (Honestly, a lot of the time, it's because we may not even know ourselves!) Typically, the conversation consists of:

"Mommmmmm, I want a phone!"

"Fine, you can have a phone."

"Yayyyy!"

"Just make sure you only use it for emergencies, and I don't wanna see you on it 24/7."

"Ok."

That is usually it. We all know the reality of how that kid uses it is much different. So, we don't train our kids how to use the phone properly, and we don't pay for classes to help them understand social media and the implications of using it. Instead, we just hand it to them and let them figure it out on their own.

Often times, what happens is that our kids get picked on in school, and it ends up on social media. That is the first inkling that something is up with this whole social media thing. What happens, every so often, is that it escalates from there. Sadly, there are even a few times when something that happens on social media ends up in the death of a child.

Whether it's a predator on an application like KIK who ends up killing a young girl (which recently happened on the East Coast), or the pressure of students harassing others online so much that they end up hurting themselves, harm can happen online when we don't train and teach kids how to use social media properly. It is like handing them a loaded gun and hoping for the best.

We have to stop handing our kids a loaded phone with all the apps and things they want and then wondering why it blows up in our (and their) faces. We have to start learning how to use some of these things ourselves, so that we aren't surprised when something happens. Even if it's just the settings in each application so that we know how to hide our kid's location or private information from anyone who is lurking as a predator.

I don't mean to be dramatic with the metaphor, and I know that it might sound drastic. However, to be honest, I don't think that we take social media seriously enough. We need to start changing the way we think about it if we are going to make a huge difference in our children's attitudes towards this. If we don't, we may have to utter the words "I wish I would have known...," which can be one of the worst phrases in the English language.

Boomers vs. Millennials

There is a great chasm between how the social media network is used by the Baby Boomer generation and this new Millennial generation. When I say Baby Boomers I am referring to people being born between the years 1950 and 1965. These years fluctuate a bit. However, I am envisioning my own parents, who most Millennials would call grandparents. Boomers are on social media but for vastly different reasons than their Millenial counterparts.

I mean it's free, mostly, and with the touch of a button you can generally send out a Tweet, or a picture, or a status update, essentially to the entire world. This is exciting for them, because any business proposition, or even just helpful tips and tricks for a variety of things in life, are just a click of a button away.

This means that Baby Boomers can connect on social media to long lost relatives or friends that they haven't seen for 30 years. They grew up in the day and age of writing letters or calling during the holidays to catch up on the last year of life. What an inefficient way to stay connected. However, now they can stay abreast on all that is going on (including vacations and the photos that follow) with anyone and everyone they want. They can ask their friends and family if they still have the photos they took at their wedding in the 1970s, and they can share and look at those photos the very same day online.

For the Boomers, this new level of communication is a way to expand on an existing relationship. Boomers can build new relationships online, but they tend to use social media to strengthen and connect to older existing relationships. So social media becomes an asset and really can be groundbreaking for them.

For the Millennials, it's groundbreaking in a completely new and different way. They see social media not as a way to connect to the old but rather as a way to connect and build the new. They see the potential of social media, not just for sharing photos or talking about their vacations, but as a way to make a genuine connection. For Millennials, social media is a way to feel close to someone and get to know their mind, heart and soul through comments, stories and pictures. For some of us older people, this sounds absurd, because in our day the main way you got to know someone was in person by spending time with them. However, if we really start to think back, it was not uncommon for people to get to know each other as pen pals or over handwritten letters. That was the main way people courted many years ago. So why is it more unusual that young people think they can have a relationship, or at the very least a friendship, that is based only on social media?

The truth is that they can't truly know someone until they can look in their eyes. I do believe that. However, I do know that they can create a pretty intense connection by simply chatting through direct messaging. The difference, I think, is that the pictures Millennials post or look at on Instagram, for example, are more than just photos. They believe they are looking into their friends' lives and souls and seeing what matters most to them. They are used to looking at those images and reading into the photos. They view the photos as giving them small crumbs of what is deeper within that person.

However, it is not the same with the Boomers. Those photos are simply just photos! They don't mean anything. Somebody saw something they liked and took a picture of it, so they put it up. They are still viewing everything as a way to inform people about their lives not to show them who they are. This is the major difference in the way Boomers interact with social media versus this newer generation.

We have focused on Millennials and Boomers in this section but we have left out another major group of people, US!!! The Generation X'ers that are probably the ones reading this book. We are the social media generation, because we are the ones that CREATED it. We saw the immense potential in building platforms where we could literally shrink the world and communicate with the masses. We build the book of faces, we build the grams of insta, and we created the chats that snap! The Boomer generation is playing with our technology, the Millennials are building emotional bonds with it, while we, Generation X, are ruling the world with it. We have created a whole industry that never before existed or was needed. Just search for SEO (search engine optimization) and see how many companies pop up to help you with that very thing. Talk about powerful.

This was written because of the very things my generation created. There was exciting potential and great causes that came out of our endeavors. However, there were plenty of consequences that came with it as well. We are dealing with those today. I just wanted to make sure you knew that I didn't forget about us. Generation X is an integral part of why we are where we are. We took what Boomers did and built up from there, much like Millennials will do with what we have created.

So we have to ask ourselves a question: If we don't like how Millennials are using technology, are we doing anything to change that?

We may use technology different than our younger predecessors, however, that doesn't mean that we use it appropriately and they do not! I think that is the temptation, that we look at these students with cell phones and we say, "Ha-ha, they have no lives, they always have these dang devices connected to their hands and heads." Meanwhile, we are checking our emails and writing new ones at the dinner table with our own devices. The message about social media and the issues that come with it are not just for Millennials or for students of today: it is for all of us.

Computer screen time, as well as cell phone screen time, is linked to a host of issues which includes sensory overload, according to Psychology Today. This doesn't even address all the physical problems including neck, back and eye issues. So, if we are on our devices constantly checking emails or playing Candy Crush, we can't very well come down with the hammer on our kids when they are checking Instagram, Snapchat and any other social media application.

We have to ask ourselves: What messages are we sending our kids about social media? How are we using our devices? And what impact is it having on those around us? When we are able to answer these questions honestly, we can start the conversation with our younger generations about how we can help them to see the same things.

> *Twitter has the operational capacity to handle 18 Quintillion user accounts.*
>
> **-Venture Beat
> (Shewan, 2017)**

Actual Hardware

Each phone application presents its own set of issues and dangers as well as benefits. Sometimes, this is where we get tripped up because there are so many apps, and it can be so tough to keep on top of the new things that are constantly coming out. We have to be vigilant, and yet it can be tough. Whenever I hear about a new app out there that kids might be using, I make it a point to download it and play around with it so that I can figure out all the ways it's meant to be used and in what ways teens can misuse it.

For example, apps like Twitter and Facebook are obvious ones that teens use, and we should figure out how those applications were originally intended and how they are most often used.

Additionally, do you know how to set and reset privacy settings on these? Can you tell me how to find the different variety of hashtag posts on both? The average person would probably struggle with one or more of these questions. So if that is the case, how much harder is it to understand applications you may not have even heard of…ones like Snapchat, WhatsApp, Yik Yak, Kik, musical.ly, etc. (By the time you are reading this, these may not even be around anymore, but a whole new set will have come out to take their place.)

Learning new apps may seem daunting at first, but they have something in common. They all have a *Settings* button, some are hidden throughout the app, but they all have them, and that is where you can decide who sees what on your profile or in your messages.

Settings in most apps look like this:

Some of these apps, like Periscope (which is a live-streaming video app), show other people your exact location on a map while you are live videoing. That can be pretty unnerving if it is a child who is using the app. I have a colleague and friend who loves putting on what she calls *life labs*. That is where an educator or parent comes to a meeting with all the apps downloaded that they have found on a teen's phone. Then, they sit around opening and playing with those apps together, discussing things that they find and ways that it can be used. It's a great way to empower a parent to really feel safer and ready to deal with all the things that the app could bring for their kids and their friends. It truly is the best way to be in the know. If we aren't interactive with our phones and the social media that our kids are using, we may be left behind in a lot of the areas of need and struggle with those apps. The only foolproof way to protect kids is to work to understand their apps thoroughly. Plus, then we know when our kids are trying to pull a fast one on us!

The Space

I had an amazing opportunity to speak a few weeks ago at Yale University, which was an honor. I talked to a group of Connecticut teachers about the topic, "Minds of Boys and Girls." During that time, we talked about social media and a discussion came up about what sort of a space the Internet had become. Someone stated, "Since adolescents are all about learning boundaries, isn't the social media world a safe place to find those boundaries since it's virtual." Another teacher raised her hand and said, "It's not a safe place because the actions are so immediate. And since the frontal lobe in a teen's brain isn't done maturing, they aren't posting wisely, which makes it a dangerous space."

So which is it?

A dangerous or a safe place for teens to explore themselves and their networks?

For me the answer is BOTH. It is both a dangerous and a safe place, simultaneously. I mean, the social media space is just a space. It is neither dangerous nor safe.

WE are the ones who decide whether it is safe or not. We can make it a safe place, and we can allow it to be a dangerous place. It's up to us.

Teens are at an age where their brain is changing and developing along with their emotions and hormones. So, they do need to test boundaries and figure out who they are and what they think about an infinite amount of topics. (This is typically why they are always right.)

In a lot of cases, I think we do our kids a disservice. They say things like "I'm in love!" or "You don't know what this feels like." To an extent, they are exactly right. See, their brains are feeling that rush of chemicals when they fall in love for the first time ever. They have never had or felt that sensation before, so for them it really is INTENSE! They can't think about anything else, and they don't know how to act or react to anything.

Truth be told, we were there too once upon a time, but for some of us, we've felt that feeling so many times over the years that we have become a bit jaded. So when our teen comes crying to us about a feeling of love, we roll our eyes and tell them that they will just get over it. That is not only doing them a disservice but it is disrespectful to everything they are feeling.

Sometimes, it doesn't surprise me that our teens are going to strangers online to ask for advice, or that teens feel like they are able to talk to someone online more than they can talk to their parents. We can be very dismissive of what they are going through. For most of us over the age of 35, we didn't grow up with technology as prevalent as this current generation. So we, in a lot of ways, don't know what it's like for them. We should be humbled and looking to help out where we can instead of the eye rolls…I mean, hey, we don't like it when they do it to us!

Tips and Tricks

The 5 things you can do instead of saying "no" to social media for your child.

The scenario is all too familiar:

"Can I have a Twitter account?"

"No, you are too young!"

"Can I have a Facebook account?"

"Nope!"

"Wellllllll …can I have a phone to play games on?"

"Sure!"

I know this is not the way it typically goes, however, the end result is still the same. Parents are continuously saying no to social media access for their children. Yet, their kids are still finding a way to get online, and they are starting their own pages and accounts with countless social media applications.

> ***71% of teens use more than one social networking site.***
>
> **-PEW Research Center (Shewan, 2017)**

As an educator, I have had to help discipline teens who have had altercations with other teens, and more and more, they tell me that it started online. Surprisingly, when I bring up the social media piece to the parents, I get the same answer, "I don't allow my child to have social media, so that can't be right...." Kids are finding ways to get online, regardless of what parents want.

I propose an alternative...instead of constantly saying "no" .... why don't we say "YES"?!

Say YES to the nagging, say YES to letting them choose independence and say YES to leave us alone!! Well, maybe not quite all of that. But there can be easier ways to manage your kids' social media...

1. Friday Fun Night!

Have a family social media night, Facebook Fridays, Twitter Tuesdays, or Instagrammmmm.... Ok, I can't think of anything that goes cleverly with Instagram. Once or twice a week, while the family is sitting around the dinner table (or, in my house, the television), yell out FACEBOOK FRIDAY! The last one to grab their device, and prove they have the Facebook app open, has to go first. Then go around the room and have each person share what they are seeing on their Facebook feed. What is happening in their digital universe? Now, the next person shares...and so on. While they are sharing, talk about what you are hearing, engage them in discussions. That way, their private apps no longer become secrets, or something they feel they must hide. Instead, they become opportunities for conversations and for suggestions on whether to like or comment on something. By talking about these things openly and having everyone share, you will be amazed at what you learn about your kids and how open and honest they will be.

2. Workshops and Training

Have a training day! Everyone needs it. Anytime we start a job we have weeks of training. However, when it comes to social media, where we share personal information for the world to see, we have less, if any, training on what is socially acceptable and appropriate. So, make Saturday mornings a training session. Use that as a time where all your children sit around with their social media open (either on a tablet or their phones), and talk about what to post, how to post, and what makes something too much information (or not enough) in your family. This goes both ways…have your kids teach and train you about new apps they are hearing about. Read the reviews online together and decide as a group whether an app is useful or not. Your family may decide that Twitter suits your needs over Instagram…or the other way around. Make these decisions together.

3. Bring the secret out into the communal.

Much like every other technology advancement, when we first bring it home, we quickly become a little obsessed with it. This is normal and happens all the time. When I got that Nintendo we were talking about earlier, I would sneak out of my room at night and creep out to see what my parents were doing in the living room, usually they were busy playing against each other on a video game!

That is why at night, before bed, all phones, tablets, pagers, laptops, etc. go in the "charging box". The charging box goes in the parent's bedroom or closet, and the electronics inside get plugged in to charge, but they are all turned off. I have found that teens or kids that take their phones to bed with them are more likely to post at night, obviously. However, those posts, and even texts, get riskier and riskier as the night gets later. No good text goes out at 2 am. And, as a dear friend tells her students, "Nothing good happens at a sleepover...ever!" So lock it up at night to make sure that your kids are learning not to obsess and overuse their new social media apps.

4. Hand out/Phone out

I have a good friend, who once a week at random days and times will come to her children and simply hold out her hand. The children place their phone or device in her hand, and she opens it up and casually looks at their messages, their posts, contacts and especially their pictures. If they have a code on their phone she makes them take it off, or it has to be an agreed upon code, so that she can gain access at all times. Otherwise, they lose privilege of the device. I think that having random checks doesn't seem to be a bad thing as long as they are consistent and fair. Ask questions about what you find, and give your child a chance to explain anything. This helps give them a voice and use critical reasoning skills.

5. Double OOOOOOO 7

If all else fails, there are plenty of spy applications and computer programs that you can install in their devices so that you know all of the things they are doing when you are not around. This might seem a bit anti what you are trying to teach…but, then again, we were the kids whose mom drove behind them while they walked to the bus stop, just to make sure we got there safe. So, I am all about putting in safety nets so that I can step in if, and when, I see danger. I recommend you take a deep breath and remember (or research) what is age appropriate while you look through their social media. Sometimes, what seems out of line to you may be fairly normal for their age group and maturity level.

We don't have to say no when there are logical and simple reasons why we could say yes. Yes, we will have to be engaged more and stay on top of our own digital game (so to speak), but that is a great thing to do anyways. At the end of the day, you paid (what?) $600 for a phone or $400 for a tablet or however much you p[aid. You also pay a hundred bucks a month for service for that device. You are giving your children over a grand to play with (and use) per year. Don't you think you have every right to know everything that is on that device? How it works? And how it's being used? I think so. Which is why I want you to feel the power to say "YES" more!

Tips and tricks for when teens/tweens/even us adults cross the line on social media

1. "I am so disappointed in you"

Do not use SHAME. For many parents, when they hear that their kid has done something unfortunate online, whether it is posting a statement that could be seen as bullying or sending photos of a lewd nature, they respond by shaming the child. Students are going to mess up and make bad choices online. We know this is going to happen. How do we know? The same reason we know we need to use timeout for 2-year-olds. Because they are going to test and push boundaries. How else will a teen learn how to think for themselves or figure out the consequences of their actions and what they mean?

This is why communication between adults and teens is so crucial. That way teens know that what they are going through is normal and that they can come to us when things happen. If we yell or talk down to our kids and make them feel ashamed about what they have done, then they are more likely to continue the very actions you are trying to change.

2. No matter what you do, children will listen…

Listening is key! Asking them why they made that choice, and then listening and understanding what they have to say can help them learn more than any yelling or grounding will. I agree that we wish they wouldn't have made that choice, and we can even be disappointed in them. However, that is not going to help them learn or change any type of behavior. So, talking about what happened, listening to them, and coming up with strategies of what should change in the future are really all we can do.

Whether they are seeking someone's approval or wanting a boy/girl to like them, that is what we teachers call a "teaching moment." So teach them…it's no different than when we were kids and we made a bad decision at a party and the next day everyone at school knew about it. We wished we could've had someone to talk to us about it. Or maybe we didn't make that choice at all. But putting ourselves in the shoes of our teens is empathy, and that is something we should give freely and often, especially to our own students and teens!

3. Boundaries are the fence posts of life

Once something like this happens, we have no choice but to move on from it. So, let's say that our 14-year-old girl, in an effort to please some boy at school, sends him a picture of herself that is either lewd or... let's just say doesn't show her in a positive light. A nude perhaps. After that, the boy decides to send it around at school. So now our 14-year-old has a bad reputation. (I wish I could say that this story is farfetched or made up, but I hear this exact story in almost every state I go to from hundreds of parents and educators.)

We have to sit with our girl and decide from now on what are we going to do. In the future, when someone asks us for something similar, what are we going to say? When someone makes a comment at school, what is she going to respond with? Should you meet with her teachers or the boy's parents? These are the boundary questions that we all need to sort through together, so that this experience is a learning one and not a tragic one.

If we continually allow our kids to change schools or move classes instead of dealing with this head on, they will never get to a point where they have the tools to stand up for themselves and become more resilient in the process, which is our ultimate goal.

4. We can all use a little bit of vision

There's a great book I've been checking out lately. It's called *How to Raise an Adult* by Julie Lythcott-Haims. The premise of the book is to imagine what kind of a 30-year-old you want your child to be. Work backwards from there to see how you should raise that child in order to get that type of an adult.

It's a great idea. In fact, I think that we need to let our students join us in that conversation. Asking them, "What kind of adult do you want to become?" "When you are 30 how do you see yourself, and what are you like?" Let them cast that vision and then ask them what you can do to support them in making changes to become that type of person. More often than not they are wanting to be successful. So talking about what they have done online that is hurting that success more than it's helping it.

Using this approach is much more productive and engaging for our students. We will see better results when we come at it this way as opposed to simply telling them to "never do it again."

5. Shut it down!

As a last resort, if they are unable to understand why what they did was wrong or they continually make similar or worse mistakes online, you may be forced to take drastic measures. It may get to a point where we don't want the mistakes to continue, but unfortunately our kiddos are not in the same agreement.

This is when we need to shut it down. That's right, we may have to take a timeout (or give them a timeout) from social media. I don't suggest any type of overreaction. Rather, let them know that a break needs to happen, and then we delete all the social media off of their devices. Not just logout to login later, but delete it altogether. If, and when, it is safe or boundaries are understood, then they can start a brand new account (one with better people as friends).

If we pay just a few bucks extra on our wireless plan, we can know at any time what apps are on all of our devices on that same plan. Again, I don't recommend that we do this behind our kids backs, not at all, we do it with their full knowledge and tell them that we will be there to help them make sure they don't keep making poor choices. We are on their side, and we want them to win. However, taking the object away that they are hurting themselves with (whether it is the app or the phone) may be the best way to help them in the long run.

If we take steps to show them we have their best interest in mind, they will respond. Maybe not in the timeframe we would like. (I know, even for me, I didn't realize all my parents had done for me until I went away to college.) We are playing the long-term goal game though, not the short term, so if worse comes to worst, Shut it DOWN!

Tips and Tricks on how to brand yourself online

Branding yourself is a concept that has been reserved primarily for businesses and life coaches. It is talked about in board meetings, at company conferences and in the living rooms of aspiring entrepreneurs. Branding does not have to stop there, however. To be able to decide what we want others to see about us online can be a powerful thing.

If we can teach others how to brand themselves online and use the power of social media to show others who we are (in positive ways), then we aren't using social media for negative things. If a student is building an online digital e-portfolio, then they aren't worried about who didn't tag them in a post or who called them a name on Twitter. If we are going to harness this idea of branding ourselves, we need to ask ourselves a few questions.

1. Who are you?

The first question we should all ask ourselves every morning when we wake up: Who are we?

We have to begin to define ourselves. I don't mean this on an existential level. I mean we have to come up with a motto, a life statement, if you will. Let me give you an example, for my business when I speak, my goal is to "make audiences laugh, reflect and grow." It's really up to you to decide what that statement is, whether it's something as simple as "live, laugh and love" or specific to your faith or what your family holds dear. It doesn't have to be your own creed. It can be one that you've heard and admire.

Once you decide what it is, everything you post, share or like on any social media should be looked at through that lens. This should be the first thing that is thought about before posting, regardless of which social media you are opening. So, in this example, I only post things, like things, or share things that help people "laugh, reflect and grow." This is the start to branding yourself online.

2. What are you doing?

The second step to branding yourself is to begin looking at what you are currently doing. What are you spending your time with? Are you volunteering? Are you doing sports or working on academics? Are you throwing yourself into your job? What about your family? Once you begin answering these questions, you should also begin posting these things as well.

Post about the things that are currently going on…the awards you are winning, the grades you are getting and the accolades you are getting at work. These posts can help people from the outside understand what is important to you. All the while, you are still using the lens of your motto or life creed to post them through.

3. Where are you going?

Once we have successfully navigated the first two questions, we have to begin to ask ourselves the third: Where are we going, and what do we want our future to look like? If our goal is college, we should be thinking and posting about what steps we are taking to get there. Or, if our goal is a career of some sort, then we should take steps to post and discuss what we are going to do to achieve that goal as well.

This is how we paint a picture of how we are moving small pieces and taking baby steps to make those futures a reality. This is a culmination of our life goals and what we are currently doing. Those two things should be leading us to our future and helping us visualize, and verbalize with social media, where our next stop is on the success train.

4. What do you stand for?

One of the most important questions is what things you are passionate about. What do you care about enough to work towards making it better for everyone in your community? Body image issues? Bullying? World hunger? World peace? You have to decide what your passion is and what you want to tell the rest of the world about in order to raise awareness. This is something that you should be posting and discussing on your social media accounts as well. Just make sure that you know what your passion is first. Posting about too many things, too many times, can be confusing to your audience.

Answering these four questions and having our posts really only focus on them, and them alone, is a great way to brand ourselves. We have an instant digital portfolio that we can present to a university, a nonprofit or a company so that they can better know us in a healthy way. It has become a great asset instead of a liability.

We keep hearing about situations where someone didn't get hired, or got fired, because of something they have done on social media…let's flip that around and let social media be the reason we got a job or even a raise. When we are focused on using it as a tool, we are no longer fighting with other people on it or getting upset at what other people are posting. Let's choose the positive and, instead of ignoring or withdrawing from Social Media, utilize it to make us and those around us better!

Summing It All Up

I fully understand that this mini-book is a lot to digest, and it may take a few reads to see what you are able to implement with your families or students.

The biggest issue is how we are going about correcting what is happening online…it's the heart of the issue I want to address and help fix, even if the specifics change day by day. If we spend all of our time putting out the small fires that happen, we will never have the energy we need to create a healthy and safe space for our kids and teens to explore and enjoy.

In this book, you will find a few ideas on how you can feel safer and more confident when you address social media with the teens and students in your life. Whether you are a parent, an educator, a therapist, all of those combined or something else entirely this book is supposed to be simply a jumping off point to begin the discussions that we all need to start having. How can we make the digital reality safer and more meaningful to the people we care about in the physical reality we find ourselves in?

It doesn't have to be, nor should it be, a crusade to clean up the Internet, but rather, it should be a learning process so that we can pass on knowledge to our children with our words and with our actions. That way they know that we are doing our best to learn alongside them.

Social media seems like an insurmountable space, and trying to run down and understand each and every app is tireless. If we try to control it all, we will be exhausted and risk breaking a healthy relationship with our kids. It's not about controlling anything. It's all about taking one step forward to understand a bit more about social media and our Millennials each day. If we keep taking those small steps, we can eventually look back and see the long way that we have come. It is that sort of mentality that will aid us in the digital age that consumes us.

References

Shewan, D. (February, 2017). "47 Social Media Facts to Blow Your Mind." *The WordStream Blog*. Retrieved February 2017 from www.wordstream.com/blog/ws/2015/11/13/social-media-facts

Vitelli, R. (February, 2014). Are There Benefits to Playing Video Games? Psychology Today. Retrieved December 2016 from www.psychologytoday.com/blog/media-spotlight/201402/are-there-benefits-in-playing-video-games

Glossary for Technology Norms

This is typically where I give you all sorts of app names and tech terms that you can reference. The only issue is that the week after I write these down, they will change. There is so much to keep up on. So, instead of making it your job (or my job) to make sure that we know about every single app that comes out and the impact it might have on kids, I thought it would be better if I simply told you about some amazing resources that I have found. If you have searched on the Internet for apps that manage apps, you would find quite a few options, so I'm going to limit this to the ones that I personally like. BUT, please do your own research, and find one that works for your family, specifically. I know many Internet providers and cell phone companies are coming up with new and great ways to keep track of the apps that are used in your home.

The first one that I have used, and really like, is a website called Safe, Smart, & Social. It provides readers with an app guide and a video that discusses all the apps in detail and explains whether they fall into the green, grey or red category, depending on how safe they are for your kids. What is even more awesome about this website is that you can sign up to receive a weekly Internet check on your kid's social media impact. The website searches the Internet for your kid's impact and reports it back to you! It's a quick and easy way to stay on top of things. I like this website a lot, and it seems to have been really helpful to a lot of people.

The second one that I like, and have suggested, is called Circle with Disney. This one does cost some money. But, strangely enough, you can order a device which helps you control all the devices in your home. If you want your child to only be able to spend 30 minutes on Facebook, the app lets you control that. If you want to shut off your Internet while you sleep, that is also possible. This is a really neat tool, because you can create separate profiles for each of your kids, which is especially helpful when your children are different ages and should be given different responsibilities.

These two apps are great and ones that I highly recommend. However, if you know of more, please, don't hesitate to use those.

Here's a list of a few others that I know of:

- » OurPact
- » ESET
- » Norton Family Premier
- » PhoneSheriff
- » Net Nanny

I am always on the lookout for new, better tools that help parents cut down on the time that they need to spend monitoring their kids online. We have yet to find a tool that can do it all, but we are getting more and more advanced each day. It is a long, tough journey to start researching all the things online that are out there for our kids to find; don't go into this journey alone. There are great tools out there that can help.

About the Author

Adam is a first generation college student who has a Bachelor's Degree in Speech Communication as well as a Master's Degree in Special Education and Leadership Development. Adam is the founder of Youth Awareness and Safety. He has co-authored the book *WTF-Why Teens Fail and What to Fix* and authored the Brooks Books series featuring the bestselling mini-book *Understanding Millennials- Tips and Tricks for Working with Today's Generation*.

His consulting includes educating adults on topics such as, "The Minds of Boys and Girls" and "How to Work with Millennials", as well as a few others.

To contact Adam for speaking please go to:

www.adamleebrooks.com

To contact Adam for consulting please go to:

www.youthawarenessandsafety.org

Made in the USA
Columbia, SC
01 September 2018